Between Love and Orgasms

By William S. Friday

ISBN-13: 978-1945681998
Printed in the United States of America
Published by Silver Star Laboratory
AuthorPowered.com

To Love

What... you expected names?

Table of Contents

Better Ending

I still
believe
in the
better ending.

A Simple Phrase

I love you.
A simple phrase,
and by the way,
eternal.
Because once spoken,
it is always true.

And if a Hundred

It's not about who you want to love. Love is very much like lust in that way. If you could fuck a hundred, you could love a hundred. And if a hundred fucks, or a hundred loves, there must be a hundred reasons to love the one of them who could love you.

Will she keep you honest when you're having that asshole moment, when you don't yet know how stupid you are in those thirty seconds between your idiot words and when you speak the words that tell her you're sorry? And for those thirty seconds, will she still keep her hand on your cock, and look you straight in the eyes, waiting, because her love for you will not wane, even when it hurts her soul? And more important than that, will she tell you, right then, in that moment? Because you're a fool sometimes, and you don't want her to just get over it, you want her to share her disappointment or sadness or grief, even if, especially if, you are the one who caused it. Because that's the only way you will learn how to love.

Because only the insanity should be temporary.

It's not about who you want to love. It's about who wants to love you. And if a hundred fucks, or one. A hundred loves, or one. A hundred reasons, or one.

Your Hands

You put your hands
over my eyes
to make the day look like night,
and I saw stars.
Actual,
twinkling stars.
Silver,
in front of deepest blue.
I don't know what it means,
only that I want your hands
over my eyes,
forever.

Storm in the Desert

I do laugh, you know.
I don't let it out just anywhere, or for just anyone.
But I do laugh.

It's loud, when it's unguarded.
And sudden as a storm in the desert, or at least that's
what they tell me a storm in the desert is like.
I wouldn't know
any more than most folks would know my laugh.
But I bet, one day, you'll know both.

Absolution

She said...
Baby,
I wanna make you feel all better.
Be absolution for the blame.

I said...
I appreciate that
Lover.
But I no longer play the game.
I won't give myself that freely now,
or ever be the same.
I don't let my guard down,
because you haven't earned my pain.
And there is no absolution
for the blame.

Always

The night December came
In the second week of spring
And on this night
I realized that always
Does not wait for
The pages of the calendar to turn
And a year's obligations be fulfilled

Spring is as much always
As December
As much always
As a grapefruit in July
Always is everything
And everything is always

Happy is always
Sad is always
Joy and sorrow
Love and hate
Are always
Just the same

You and I were always

From the first time we spoke
When one made the other saddest
We stayed always

When the other made the one angriest
Always we remained
In the moment you showed your teeth
And called me a liar
There was no end to always
Because always doesn't leave

Tell the sand on a beach
That it is no longer there
While the high tide obscures it from view
Time and tides move
But always waits in place
Secure
In darkness

Tell the sun it has left the sky
When the ground has only turned its face away
Until the next new
Dawn of always

Sand and tide are always

Sun and ground are always

You and I are always

Bargained with God

As you lay there,
I bargained with God
for you to be okay.
I told God I would give up
all rights and claims on you
if he would allow you to be well,
and live a long and happy life without me.
And God said,
"Didn't she already break up with you?"

Breathing

I don't overshare.

Yes, I have thoughts. Yes, I have feelings. No, I don't put them out there, all heart on my sleeve, for the world at large to see and sift through. I had that, in no uncertain terms, kicked outta me years and years ago by someone I loved, and that was enough for one lifetime. Of course now, it's taken as a sign of unwillingness on my part to be intimate, but whatever. It's my sleeve, and I'll leave it bare if I want to.
A while ago, I mastered the art of Vaguebooking, but was told, in equally certain terms, that behavior like that only alienates folks from getting to know the real me, but for me, it's easier to speak the truth I know people want to hear, or just say nothing at all. Again, the feelings are there, I've just been conditioned to keep them to myself.

It doesn't make for many friends or lovers, but I've become reconciled with that, believing, until recently, that when it comes to pain in the heart places, less is better.

Yeah, I said "until recently".

See, I've been going through a fuck-ton of things in the last year, and thought I could poet my way through them. Thought I could silent my way

through them. Thought I could Vaguebook my way
through them.

I've been going through a fuck-ton of things in the
last year, and I had to finally say something. The
only way I know how. After the fact.

A friend of mine, a really good friend, recently told
me something that, in the moment, froze my bones.

That something was,
"With change comes sacrifice."

I didn't say it in that moment, but I truly hated those
words. Things had been changing so rapidly in my
life that the last thing I wanted to hear was that,
with all this change, I was going to have to "sacrifice" something or somethings I still held onto like
a cheap life jacket after the leaky boat sinks. I was
barely hanging on as it was, and NOW comes sacrifice?

On a seemingly unrelated note, a few weeks before
this, I had begun the practice of spoken affirmations.
Not the kind you might think, but the kind that only
I would think to practice. Notice I did not say posi-
tive affirmations. I began the practice of negative affirmations. With phrases like,

"I wish I had never met you."
"I need to get you OFF of me."
And most recently,
"You're somebody else's problem now".

Whenever I began to feel the sink of sadness begin
to drag me to the hell of my own dark mind, I would
invoke those, and other phrases. These negative
affirmations became my talismans against the feelings that kept me from moving. They allowed me
the freedom of expression that Vaguebooking never
could. They created in me the ability to breathe.
Not in, but out. And this was important for me to
understand, because, in the world of breathing, you
learn quickly that your life is only as good as your
next breath. And if you spend your life holding one
breath, that breath just might kill you, because you
have to breathe out to breathe in the next breath,
and the next, and the next.

You have to sacrifice that breath if you ever hope to
have another.
So in my mind, I did.

And shortly after that, I had me a day. The kind
where you wake up one way, and if you just keep
breathing, it ends different than you thought it
would.

You see, I woke up holding my breath. Then sometime during that day, I sacrificed that breath for the promise of the next breath, and the next, and the next. And the words in the picture at the top of this page were that day. Poeted through. With the promise that there could be more than just holding my breath, waiting for the next breath to come.

Somewhere on Facebook, maybe a little, but not in a way I think will be held against me, I posted these words, and Instagram posts, at the end of that day, "Today, I wrote myself all the way through a sadness that has hung on me, like grave clothes, since last fall. These are the trilogy of Instagram posts that were the path for those feelings to find their way out..."

There is no snappy conclusion to this post. One that ties up all the loose ends of all the thoughts I've just unloaded on you who read this. It's like life, I guess.

It's just a series of breaths that keep you going along the way to more life, and the next breath, and the next, and the next. And now that I've finally let go of that one breath I've held for so long, sacrificed it for the change to come, I know I'm still breathing. And that's living.

Broken

I'm too broken
for some,
and not broken enough
for others.

Circus

I would
run away from home
to join
your circus.

Catalyst

There's a poignancy to changes in an ingrained life, lived flawed, but still true to human nature. Change is not natural, and it only comes by way of trauma, either physical or emotional. And though the choices for our changes are brought about under the sovereign hand of our autonomy of spirit, there is always a catalyst, and never one of our choosing. I am no different than any other soul that must change.

My catalyst is emptiness.

For me, it was a two-step process. First you lose most of what you have, and then, you give the rest of it away. The losing isn't all that hard. Humanity is conditioned to lose. It's what we do most of the time. We're used to it from as far back as our earliest memories. It's the real reason we idolize winners. A winner is humanity's real life superhero. They succeed where the rest of us fail, and we idolize them because of it. To be human is to worship, and it is easiest to worship the demigod who looks like a better version of us. Hero worship is as real a thing as hunger and thirst, and easier to satisfy. Just find a winner and put your hopes on them, while all of us who aren't them keep doing what we do best.

Lose.

But after the losing comes the hard part. The giving away of whatever you have left. You're already a loser. Not a day goes by when you aren't reminded of it. For most, the response is to try and hold fast to what's left of your losses. For the rest, there is a different choice.

I used to be that guy who held on. To everything. Until there was nothing left to hold onto. Until life removed the last of everything I thought I want-ed. And the thing you realize when everything you thought you wanted isn't yours anymore, is that you can finally let go of the rest.

So after a life of losses, now comes my time to let go, because only empty hands can take hold of the good that comes after defeat.

And I'm going to need a new catalyst.

A Funny Way

She had a funny way of
showing how she missed me,
running away just as fast
as she could,
and usually right after
telling me so.
But here's the thing.
I always missed her
when I told her so.
I just hoped she could have
missed me too.

Promise to a Lady

I made a promise to a lady not to die.
At least not before she did.
But one day,
I'm going to break that promise.
And I know it will kill her,
as surely as it killed me
to make it.

Community Property

How can you
reclaim
something for
yourself
that was never yours
alone?

Crazy

Don't get me wrong,
I got a thing for
Crazy.

Crazy
dives headfirst into everything.

Crazy
lets you know there's nothing wrong with you,
as long as you see nothing wrong with
Crazy.

Crazy
fucks on the second date,
sometimes even if you play your cards wrong.
Sometimes,
because you play your cards wrong.

Crazy
takes you out of yourself.

Crazy
takes you with it,
even if you don't want to go.

Crazy
doesn't care how comfortable you are,
because
Crazy
wants to show you a good time,
possibly the best time you've ever known.
And the thing with
Crazy
is,
all you have to do is say yes.

Echoes

My body stirs
again
in the echoes
of you.

Despicably

I want
to do
despicably
beautiful
things
to you.

Gutter

I will love you
from the gutter,
to the stars,
and back.

Drinking Alone

The problem with
drinking alone
is not so much the
drinking, as
the alone.

December

When I finally
give up,
will you cry
over me?

Empty-handed

One extra pair of shoes is all I'm taking with me in my duffel bag. A couple pairs of jeans, some tee shirts, and a coat for when a cold wind starts to blow. Because the unlined bed of my pickup truck is not for junk, but for sleeping. And furniture won't fit except to leave it by the curbside when I go.

I'm gonna move on, empty-handed. Live life as intended. Value people over things, accept today for what it brings, and when tomorrow is ended, I'll be gone.

The strain upon my back from carrying so many things was a burden. The weight of the unnecessary only served to bend my narrow frame. But surviving for this long gave me the time it took to learn the lessons. That there is no guilt, no fault, no shame. And if I don't let go, I have only me to blame.

I'm gonna move on, empty-handed. Live life as intended. Value people over things, accept today for what it brings, and when tomorrow is ended, I'll be gone.

Just because my hands are empty doesn't mean that they aren't scarred. And another hand to hold is not a burden, but a blessing. If you'll put your hand in mine, life may be hard, but we'll be fine.

A beautiful tomorrow is not guaranteed, any more

than the past was worry-free. But I choose to take my chances on a future with no plans, as you can see. Because this is moving day, and life will never be the same. My slate is clean, my tether cut, and if I hesitate, I have only me to blame.

I'm gonna move on, empty-handed. Live life as intended. Value people over things, accept today for what it brings, and when tomorrow is ended, I'll be gone.

Every Time

I can write pretty words
while thinking of you,
and in the repeating of them hear,
in my mind,
the echo,
"fuck you",
every time.

Little Black Book

I gave you all away today.
I know how funny that must sound,
because none of you knows
that the others exist.
But you did exist,
Until I gave you all away.
All of you but one.

Love Poems

I'm sorry I won't be writing
any love poems,
because I would have loved writing
those most of all.

You Are

You are loved by me.
Not in ways that are expected,
nor celebrated by the masses.
But you are loved by me.
This love so seldom given to any,
and only by my choice.

You are loved by me,
and that is rare.
This love that is tender,
but not soft.
Gentle,
but not weak.
Formed by life to hold and uphold,
comfort and give strength.
To make alive and to give peace.

You are loved by me,
and most won't understand.
This love that can be violent,
but not as violence is understood in those who are,
by their nature,
violent.
And always only outwards.
Never towards the ones on whom my love rests.
Outwards,
towards any who seek to harm you,
or they,

the few.

You are loved by me,
This love that is not revolutionary,
for that would be to call it something the world has
not seen.
This love is only as it should be,
and that is to call it what love is.
What you will always see.

/

Madness

Then you say to yourself,
"What if this really IS madness,
and I'm just good at it?"

Healing

The only thing
healing
my past
is the future.

I Dreamed

I took a nap.
I dreamed.
Something good happened.
I woke up.
I was never there.

Movies and Baseball

I don't have the answers.
I used to. Then I didn't.
And now,
I know I never will again.
So,
don't look to me for them.
Avoid using sentences that
end in question marks when we talk.
Keep your own counsel.
Let's just talk movies and baseball.
Okay,
just movies.
And kiss me when you go.

I Forgive You

It occurred to me today
that I have never
forgiven anyone,
for anything,
ever.
I might have said,
"I forgive you",
but now I know
that was a lie.
I forget,
I don't forgive.
I don't think I can.
I don't think I know how.
And I don't think
I'm changing.

My Father's Laugh

It was my father's laugh coming out of me.
The one I would hear when I got a little older than
childhood.
The one I heard when he and my mother would do
random things together in public.
The one that made me know how much he loved her.

Low

It's lonely in here.

I've never had a problem with being my own company. I've kept it my entire life without any complaint.

But now, I finally realize what being alone means.

The new of being without someone has sunk in, and I understand what it is to miss another human.
My human.

I won't beg. I won't act desperate in the company of others. And I sure as fuck won't settle for something less than I deserve.

But tonight my standards are low, and I'm drinking.

No Tengo

I ain't got the one thing I need,
'cuz
the one thing I need ain't a thing.
I got over-priced shelter, and under-priced food,
'cuz
this is motherfucking America.
I got the right to vote, unhindered,
'cuz
my ancestors bugged outta northern Europe with
only the white skin on their backs.
I got a job that allows me the freedom that comes
from seventy-hour weeks, and no vacations.
I got clothes and shoes,
'cuz
an inexhaustible workforce makes them for me, then
dies early and poorly for my privilege to wear other
peoples' names on them.
Names that are not forgotten, like those of the children who stitched this shit together.
I got a small TV and a computer that calls itself a
cellphone,
'cuz
without them I would not know what it is I'm told I
need.
And I got fading memories,
'cuz
the things that stay with me longest can only be
saved and stored in a bucket made of bone, on a

hard-drive more revered by hungry zombies than by
the living.
But I ain't got the one thing I need,
'cuz
the one thing I need ain't a thing,
'cuz
the one thing I need is you.

Just Human

A day for reflection,
about the past,
sure,
but more about the present.
I am loved,
and I am hated.
That doesn't make me special,
just human.
All that matters to me now is,
who is doing the loving,
and who is doing the hating.
And fuck to the future,
until tomorrow.

Forward On

If by winter,
she would be.
Alone with you,
eternal we.
Then there are things
that I must do,
to show her that
she wants this me.
And forward on
that day to see.

And forward on
that day to see.

I do not know
the why right now.
The who, the what,
the questions how.
But on this day
one thing I do,
when winter comes
it shall be so.
And forward on
with life we'll go.

And forward on
with life we'll go.

2 December 2016

I gave up hope today.
You didn't notice because you were too busy remembering the past to see us lose our future.
But today was when it happened.
I even wrote this so one of us would never forget.

Not the Same

Never was
is not the same as
never will be.
But never was,
and never was to be,
is.

Everything I Say

I mean everything I say.
And sometimes,
I change my mind.

Feral Puppy

Love is a feral puppy,
hiding in the crawl space
under the house you were raised in.
At once growling,
then whimpering,
simply asking to be found.

Notches

There are no notches on my bed.
I've never been that guy.
Notches scar my heart, instead.
And I don't even try.

Fucker

I wanted to write screenplays,
except,
it turns out,
I don't have the discipline
for things that take more than
fifteen minutes to complete.
Except for sex.
Unlike writing,
I could do that all day,
or night,
depending.
So,
while despising the name,
I became a poet.
The same way,
while despising the name,
I became a lover.
They're both just names,
basically,
for the same thing.
Fucker.

Giggle

I heard you giggle.
All the way on the other side of the room,
I heard you giggle.
I heard you giggle,
and I wanted to know what they said to you.
I wanted to know what they said to you that could
cause such a beautiful sound fill the air.
To fill my soul.
I wanted to know what they said to you,
so I could say it better.
Better,
so that my words could fill your soul.
I heard you giggle.
It started as a laugh,
a good laugh,
a warming laugh.
Until it was something more.
Something higher.
Higher,
like heaven is to the stars.
I heard you giggle.
All the way on the other side of my life,
I heard you giggle.
I heard you giggle,
and I wanted you to know what it did to me.
I wanted you to know what it did to me that would
cause such an uneventful life to fill and know,
that there was more of life to come.

Dialogue

"Are you okay?"

"Eh, no. I'm gonna have some
bad days...
...mixed in with all the
other bad days."

Grounded

Falling hard,
through the floorboards,
into the heart of the earth.
Together.
Grounded,
in each other.

Happy Birthday

Happy Birthday, Baby!
I thought of you today.
I surprised myself, because
I even got the date right.
I pictured you having a good time.
Then, I pictured you
fucking some guy
I will never know the name of.
Finally, I thought,
you got what you always deserved.

I Wish I'd Never

You know how there are times when you say in-side your own head in the direction of the image of someone you know, "I wish I'd never met you", but because you've seen every time-travel fantasy movie ever made, you already know that you really can't mean it because, if it came true, most of the good things in your life would have never existed?

So you take one good, deep breath, and exhale all the bad that you took inside you with that breath, and release it to whatever you tell yourself there is in the universe you believe in, just so you can get back on with what's left of this life you wish was somehow different, and you know you cannot change.

But you know how there are also times when you say inside your own head in the direction of the image of someone you know, "I wish I'd never met you", and because you've seen every time-travel fantasy mov-ie ever made, you know, since you've already taken the time to know, that it's okay to mean it because, if it came true, all the pain you're feeling right now would have never existed?

So you take one good, deep breath, and exhale all the bad that you took inside you with that breath, and release it to whatever you tell yourself there is in the universe you believe in, just because there isn't a goddamn thing in the universe that, if you didn't have it because that person never existed in your life, you could not possibly be any worse off than you are today.

Of course you know this. I just wish I had known this before it came time to say the words, inside my own head, over and over until they are not words anymore, but are like some Sanskrit mantra given me to keep my shit together in those fucked up moments between the breaths, when I whisper,

"I wish I'd never met you."

That One Thing

She had all of me,
except that one thing I never gave away,
not to anyone.
Then the day came when I was ready to give that to
her too.
And so I did,
but she called me a liar.
In all that,
I couldn't blame her,
as I took back every other thing.

The Best Joke

There are jokes,
and cosmic jokes.
But the best joke
is the one
you tell yourself
to survive.

In Other Things

The sun came out,
and it didn't burn me,
because I knew how far away to stand.
In other things,
like love,
I haven't been so lucky.

Inner Monologue

If I say this shit out loud,
I sound like a whining bitch.
And I tell myself,
"I am better than that".
But you want words.
Or do you?
Because with my words you will end us.
Maybe this is just a test.
The kind where I reveal myself to you,
only to hear your silent goodbye.
It's okay.
I already know what I am.
And I know the reasons I say so little about myself.
The uncovered me was only good enough to be
shunned by love.
Reshaped.
Painted over.
Hammered into conformity for the sake of another.
If I speak now,
I reveal all that was.
And I fear that more than I fear a life without you.

Invite Me To Your Funeral

Invite me to your funeral,
and I'll invite you to mine.
It might be unusual,
but we'll both be on time.
So let's extend the invitations,
and stick to the plan.
And we'll both be just fine,
'cause I'm a reasonable man.

Open My Mouth

"Open my mouth with yours",
he whispered,
before her lips parted,
and she slid her soul inside him.
"I have a dirty mouth",
she whispered in return.
"Then there will always be truth in your kisses",
he answered.
Before the distance between them was no more.

Worlds colliding.
Stars born then dying.
Lights fading.
Fears abating.
Hunger raging.
Salivating.
Lives in need.
Culminating.
Insanity dissipating.
No more anticipating.
Each the other's cure.

"Open my mouth with yours",
she whispered,
before their lips parted,
and their souls were at home inside each other.
"You have a dirty mouth",
he whispered in return.

"Then there will always be truth in my kisses",
she answered.
Before the distance between them was no more.

Peace

She was the first peace
I had known with another,
and looking back,
late,
too late,
I realized that my peace
had become complacency.
And when
complacency mirrored apathy,
she said goodbye.

Twin Children

Beauty and Sadness
are the twin children
of Love.

Pop Culture

I was raised on the
breadcrumbs and
bottle dregs of
pop culture.
That means you,
my dear,
are forgiven for
not getting anything I say.
You and that
big beautiful brain
of yours.

Quit

When you finally decide to
quit something,
quit it with your whole heart.
Quit the fucking shit out of it.

Rejection

I'm lying in bed,
like a whore,
asking for it,
but sleep won't
take me back.

Prize

You're a princess.
But I'm a
motherfucking prize,
so this time,
you can
sweep me off
my feet.

Remains

She took the fall for me.
I know,
because she's done it before,
for others.
This is her way.
This is what she does.
No matter what she says.
No matter how she says it.
It's in the tone of her voice.
In the look-away of her eyes.
The wordless language her body speaks
between the lines of her confession.
She absolves those she loves,
even though the guilt remains.
This I know because,
no one breaks their own heart.

Sid and Nancy and Hank

Sid Vicious was
Hank Bukowski,
if only Sid had sung
drunken love songs
to every other Nancy.

Standing Policy

I have a
standing policy of
hating the one who hurts
the one I love.
Which is why I have a
standing policy of
hating myself.

Terrible Liar

"You can love someone,
and know you're not supposed to be with them."

She had a look on her face when she said it.
And not what you'd call a straight face.
Not at all.

More like the look a person gets
when they're a really bad liar,
and they know that you know they just lied to you.

She was a terrible liar.

The Competition

I hate you,
because you've
shown me
the faults
I can't overcome.

The Consequences Of

Am I going to be lied to?
Be a part of
another person's confusion?
Their fantasy,
or escape from reality?
If I am,
then I am out.
But at least,
for just this once,
I choose to know before it is
too late,
and I,
one more time,
bear the consequences of
lying to myself,
again.

Great Happiness

The great sadness is not in the moments,
as you live them.
The great sadness is not in the years,
season after season,
as you struggle through them.
The great sadness is in the memories,
and how you now know that
the great happiness could have been yours,
in all the moments already counted,
from then till now,
that you can no longer reach.

Laughing

Dear God, I laughed today.
Not the laugh that lies,
but the laugh that can't wait
to tell the truth.
Please God, let the laughing stay.
The laughing is the sunrise.
The laughing is the hope.
The laughing is me.
I need the laughing,
and the smiling that comes with it.
Because if the laughing,
then I have come back, too.
And the girl who knew the laughing
needs to know.

Love of My Life

You used to be
The Love of My Life.
Now you're just
a love in my life.
But I still think of you,
that way,
now and then.
Reduced, but never
diminished.
Maybe thought of as
unfinished.
But you'll never know,
because I'll never open,
that part of my heart
again.

Theory of Tears

Tears don't scare me.
I know people hate them,
in themselves and in others,
depending on just how manipulated
tears make them feel.
Manipulated,
not by the tears,
but for the reasons they flow.
There is a theory of tears,
known only by a few.
Not by the ones who cry,
but by the ones who hold it in.
They have learned
all the reasons for them,
and choose not to give them away.
Unmanipulated,
and unmanipulating.
They hold onto the tears
as tightly as they do the theory.
"Tears don't scare me",
they say,
"as long as I don't have to see them."
At least that's their theory.
But the truth about
the theory of tears is this;
tears are only scary on the inside.

Timeless

Nothing says love better
than forgetting.
Because you don't exist in
each other's dates and times,
you exist in
each other's moments,
and they are timeless.

The Visitor

They spent hours on the phone together that night. Each sharing things with the other that they had either forgotten, or hadn't dreamed they'd share again with another.

And definitely not this soon.

Hours when, for her, time stopped, and she knew that on this night there would be no letting go of the thoughts she took with her to bed. She took one last look at the clock on the nightstand. It glowed 4:13 as her tired eyes shut, and she wondered how long it would take for him to visit her. One last look before her thoughts became...

There was a knock at her bedroom door, barely audible beneath the rumble of spring thunder in the distance. But there was no mistaking the sound. Patient. Insistent. One hard knuckle making a slow drumbeat against heavy wood. She raised her head from the pillow; just enough to be sure what she heard was true. As she pulled back the covers, her feet touched the hardwood floor before she knew what it was she was ready for. Walking, silently in bare feet, she reached the door and stopped. For a moment, she let the palms of her hands settle against the wood grain as her cheek pressed into the door. Three heartbeats later, she whispered,

"Is it you?"
And then, with no more hesitation, her hand found the latch, and she opened the door.
It was him.

He always loved how tall she was, and he let his eyes look her up and down the full length of her body. While he did this, her eyes never left his, knowing that when he was finished taking all of her in, he would finish with his eyes looking directly into hers. And that thought made her shiver as her pussy became like melting wax.

Before either of them could say a word, she grabbed both his shoulders with her hands, and pulled him hard against herself. The momentum she created in his body caused the two of them to crash against the wall behind her as their mouths became a crush of lips and tongues, desperate to fulfill the rising need within them. They tasted and swallowed hard at each other, as every brush of tongue on tongue, and every pinch of teeth on lips, gave more boldness to their desires. His one hand in her hair, tugging, and the other on her ass, pulling her tighter against him, she could feel just how his need of her had filled him to near-stiffness.

Gasping in muffled, high-pitched moans, her sounds

made sure he knew that what he did was right. Without thought, her hands found their way to his body. One hand around his neck, the other fumbling with his belt buckle, and then his zipper. As they kissed, her frustration at how long it was taking for her to set him free from his prison of clothes caused her to use both hands on his pants. She would not let something so cruel keep her from the part of him she wanted so badly. As she fought for what was going to be hers, he continued to follow his instincts, and her reactions, on a direct path to her pleasure. Kissing and licking her neck and shoulders, his hands found her breasts, and felt the immediate hardening of her nipples as he pressed against them through her gown. In one swift move, her hands found what they had worked so desperately for, as belt buckle and denim crashed against the wood floor.

In the moment following that sound, they stopped. Breathing heavily from exertion and lust, they held themselves still and looked once more into each other's eyes. His only words to her were,
"All of me needs all of you."

From that moment forward, there would be no more waiting.

In one motion, they swept themselves onto her bed. Whatever clothes the two of them still wore were gone in moments, leaving only the freedom of bare skin between them.

As he took her face in his hands and kissed her, wet and deep, she wrapped her hands around his hips and pulled him on top of her. They kissed like there was nothing but hunger in their hearts, air gushing in and out of them as their mouths could not settle on any one place. When her hands finally closed around his full erection, he grunted a deep sound into her open mouth, while she guided his cock between her legs, and then against her wet, swollen lips.

In disbelief, he felt both heat and a thick slickness envelop his head as she steadied him with her hands on his shaft. Responding, he lowered his mouth to her full breasts as his hands lifted them upward. His tongue felt the tightly knotted areolas, and he let himself play with them until they grew rough inside his lips.

It was then that she raised both legs, fully exposing her waiting pussy, yawned wide to take in every inch of his dangerously large member. In one moment of wordless consent for what was to come, their eyes begged for what each of them was about to do to the other. With the sudden raising of her hips, and the pull of her arms around his neck, she breathed, "Fuck me. Now."

He entered her, like falling from a great height, and landing, not in death, but into life itself.
Her cry was loud, and uncontrolled. It continued for what felt like minutes. Each new movement of him inside her caused another, and then another, moan, whimper, or throat-clenched keen to rip from her. For him, there was no end to the sensations. Every in and out, whether slow and steady, or swift and near-violent, caused wave after wave of intensity to flow from the root of his still-growing cock, to his fingers and toes. In the course of the next few minutes, he was sure he had heard and felt her first, then second, and right after that, third and fourth orgasms of the night, yet he was not ready for his. Their bodies were achieving something that could not be explained, only experienced. With every thrust he felt her contract so deep inside herself that he swore he knew when each climax would happen. For her, she had selfishly begun counting them when the third one caught her so suddenly that she thought she felt her insides pop, only to have it covered by another, and then two more, before she knew what was happening.

And as that moment passed, she looked him dead in the eyes again, and turned herself over on the bed. From her knees, she looked longingly over one shoulder, into his startled eyes, then lowered her face against the bed, and raised her ass to meet his hips and his still-engorged need. She pressed herself back into him and said, "I need you this way. Give it to me this way, hard."

And he obeyed.

Starting slowly, he felt himself slip in even deeper than he had been in before. At the point when his thrusts began to crest at the deepest parts of her, she pushed back against him even more. With every reverse thrust she gave, he heard a new sound echo out of her. Where before, there was a series of higher sounds, now what he heard were deep, guttural moans, as if she had gone from consciousness into a trance. Together, they found a new rhythm that had not been there when he was on top of her; a timing that allowed him to reach a new level of abandon with her body. At one point during this new form of play, he leaned over her and, beginning with the meat of her ass, he began to bite and claw his way upward over her back. As he bit and chewed higher and higher, her backward thrusts took over, and she controlled the force of their movements.

When she arched her back, giving him even more depth to enter, he could smell the pungent sweetness of her multiple orgasms in the air. And between the taste of her skin in his mouth, and the smell of her heat in his nose, he had lost all control. The last thing he remembered before he entered the same trance that she was in were her words, spoken over the same shoulder he had just bitten,
"As hard as you can. Cum for me. Now."

He had never given all of himself to another the way he gave himself to her in that moment. At first he couldn't tell if her sounds were from ecstasy, or from pain. He slowed himself for just a beat as if to ask if she was alright. Before he could speak, she answered,

"Don't you stop!"
And he did not stop.

The next unmeasured amount of time was, for him, a blur of moans and screams, grunts and howls. Most words failed her, but he knew everything was right when all she could say was,
"Fuck... FUCK... Yes, FUCK!"

Again and again.

For her, it was the totality of feeling and sensation. Past pleasure, through pain, and back into a pleasure she had never known before. She tried to continue the count; 11, 12, 15, until she couldn't count her orgasms any more than she could count her breaths. For him, she was that thing he never believed existed. The woman who wanted him as much as he wanted her.

For her, he was that thing she always wanted to believe existed. The man who was not afraid to be everything she always feared, and who took all her fears away.

And then, as quickly as it had all started, it ended. They collapsed onto each other, tangled, wet from sweat and juices, intertwined. Their breathing slowed, their kisses returning to a tender calm. Their bodies protecting each other from the darkest part of the night. This was their first encounter.

But not their last.

A Wish

I wish
love songs
were true.

Unrequited

Our eyes don't meet,
but I see you.
And on my best days,
I think you see me too,
or at least,
one day,
you will.
But on every other day,
I question still,
"Do you see me
like I see you?"

Your Tears

I envy your tears,
and how they come
to your rescue
when I cannot.

Wake the Sun

I got to wake the sun this morning,
from my bed of silent dreams,
in the nonsense of my plans
for another day.
I drank coffee by the window,
unnoticed in my chair.
Looking back at her,
I couldn't pull my eyes away,
but she did not see.
She'll be busy when she rises,
shining down on others through the day.
But I'll remember what she looked like
lying next to me.

Us

Each one of us
loses someone
every day.
Sometimes
we know it,
sometimes we
don't.

Warmer than a Winter

A someplace, just
warmer than a winter spent without love.
There to be,
all year 'round,
with the only one who warms me,
and steadies,
when my fear goes to ground.
Not a friend alone,
or a tender body, mere.
More than flesh and bone,
a soul so near,
my dark heart their own.

Erosion

Life wears us down
until we are smooth.
Like the crashing of
water over stones
for millennia,
life takes our beautiful,
jagged edges and,
through its persistence,
beats us clean.
Until we can't feel our
beautiful edges,
and we give in to
the comfort of the next
shallow pond.

What My Dad Saw

I have no idea
what my dad saw
in my mom,
but he was madly in love
with her.

What I Want

"Eventually,
I get what I want"
she said.

"I don't"
he thought,
in silence.

Fictionary. 8 Megapixel Artist. Bloody Awful Poet.

William S. Friday became a poet when a bad case of writer's block forced him to use smaller words, and write much shorter sentences. Bill's first full-length book, *A Death on Skunk Street*, was released in 2016. *Between Love and Orgasms* is his second book.

Bill lives on a hill overlooking the airport, near the Pacific Ocean, in Long Beach, California.

Photo Credit - Anthony Robinson

13261321R00062

Made in the
USA
Monee, IL